Delahoyde Surname

Ireland: 1600s to 1900s

From Ireland Church Records of Baptism, Marriage and Death

Comprised of Roman Catholic and Church of Ireland Records

From Counties Carlow, Cork, Kerry and Dublin City

Compiled by **Donovan Hurst**

December 10, 2012

Dedication

This work is dedicated to all of those that came before us and shaped our lives to make us the people that we are today.

Table of Contents

Introduction

This is a compilation of individuals who have the surname of Delahoyde that lived in the country of Ireland from the 1600s to the 1900s. I have placed each entry into one of four categories: Families, Individual Births/Baptisms, Individual Burials, and Individual Marriages. If a marriage entry primarily concerns an Individual Delahoyde whom is female, then I have placed that entry under the category of Individual Marriages. If a marriage entry primarily concerns an Individual Delahoyde whom is male, then I have placed that entry under the category of Families. Images of many of these listings are available at http://churchrecords.irishgenealogy.ie/churchrecords/.

To help guide the reader of this work, the format of this book is as follows:

- Main Family Entry (Husband and Wife) (Father and Mother)

  o Child of Main Family Entry, including Spouse(s) when available

    ▪ Grandchild of Main Family Entry, including Spouse(s) when available

      • Great-Grandchild of Main Family Entry, including Spouse(s) when available

(Bolded Text) following any entry includes any additional information such as Residence(s), Occupation(s), Signature(s), etc. when available.

Hurst

Some of the fonts used in this work symbolizes Celtic writing. The traditional letters, numbers, and punctuation marks and their Celtic counterparts are as follows:

Traditional Letters (Uppercase & Lowercase)

A a B b C c D d E f G g H h I i J j K k L l M m N n O o P p Q q R r S s T t U u V v W w X x Y y Z z

Celtic Letters (Uppercase & Lowercase)

A a B b C c D ð E e F f G g H ʜ I i J j K k L l M m

N n O o P p Q q R ʀ S s T t U u V ʋ W ω X x Y y Z z

Traditional Numbers

1 2 3 4 5 6 7 8 9 10

Celtic Numbers

1 2 3 4 5 6 7 8 9 10

Traditional Punctuation

. , : ' " & - ( )

Celtic Punctuation

. , : ' " & - ( )

Parish Churches
Cork & Ross
(Roman Catholic or RC)

Cork - SS. Peter & Paul Parish.

Dublin (Church of Ireland)

Glasnevin Parish, St. Audoen Parish, St. Catherine Parish, St. James Parish, St. John Parish, St. Luke Parish, St. Mary Parish, St. Michan Parish, St. Nicholas Without Parish, St. Paul Parish, and St. Werburgh Parish.

Dublin (Roman Catholic or RC)

Clondalkin Parish, Harrington Street Parish, Rathmines Parish, SS. Michael & John Parish, St. Agatha Parish, St. Andrew Parish, St. Catherine Parish, St. James Parish, St. Lawrence Parish, St. Mary, Haddington Road Parish, St. Mary, Pro Cathedral Parish, St. Michan Parish, and St. Nicholas Parish.

Families

- Barnabas (B a r n a b a s) Delahoyde & Catherine Coleman

  o Jasper Delahoyde – bapt. 1782 (Baptism, **SS. Michael & John Parish** (RC))

- Christopher Delahoyde & Lucinda Unknown

  o Mary Anne Delahoyde – bapt. 26 Jan 1800 (Baptism, **St. Mary, Pro Cathedral Parish** (RC))

  o John Delahoyde – bapt. 1802 (Baptism, **St. Andrew Parish** (RC))

  o Christopher Delahoyde – bapt. 1807 (Baptism, **St. Andrew Parish** (RC))

  o Mary Anne Delahoyde – bapt. 1812 (Baptism, **St. Andrew Parish** (RC))

- Daniel Delahoyde & Anne Cahill – 20 Nov 1768 (Marriage, **St. Catherine Parish** (RC))

  o Mary Delahoyde – bapt. 4 Dec 1770 (Baptism, **St. Catherine Parish** (RC))

- Daniel Delahoyde & Mary Carroll – 22 Oct 1787 (Marriage, **St. Michan Parish** (RC))

- Daniel Delahoyde & Mary Anne Dempsy – 16 Sep 1796 (Marriage, **St. Andrew Parish** (RC))

- Edward Delahoyde & Anne Crowley

  o Patrick Martin Delahoyde – b. 21 Apr 1890, bapt. 28 Apr 1890 (Baptism, **St. Mary, Pro Cathedral Parish** (RC))

  o Charles William Delahoyde – b. 13 Jul 1892, bapt. Jul 1892 (Baptism, **St. Mary, Pro Cathedral Parish** (RC))

Edward Delahoyde (father):

Residence - 3 Lower Gloucester Place - April 28, 1890

July 5, 1892

- Edward Delahoyde & Elizabeth Connor

  o Daniel Delahoyde – bapt. 30 Jul 1786 (Baptism, **St. Michan Parish** (RC))

- Edward Delahoyde & Isabel Connelly

  o Charles Patrick Delahoyde – b. 16 Mar 1870, bapt. 28 Mar 1870 (Baptism, **SS. Michael & John Parish** (RC))

Edward Delahoyde (father):

Residence - 10 High Street - March 28, 1870

- Edward Delahoyde & Unknown

  o Andrew Delahoyde – bur. 24 Jan 1682 (Burial, **St. Audoen Parish**)

  o Joseph Delahoyde – bur. 18 Dec 1686 (Burial, **St. Audoen Parish**)

- Frank Delahoyde & Catherine Unknown

  o Margaret Delahoyde – bapt. 17 Oct 1821 (Baptism, **St. Mary, Pro Cathedral Parish** (RC))

Frank Delahoyde (father):

Residence - Coles Lane - October 17, 1821

- George Delahoyde & Catherine Unknown

  o Elizabeth Delahoyde & Eugene Beahan – 12 Sep 1861 (Marriage, **St. Nicholas Parish** (RC))

Elizabeth Delahoyde (daughter):

Residence - Drogheda - September 12, 1861

Eugene Beahan, son of Eugene Beahan & Anne Unknown (son-in-law):

Residence - Dulick, Co. Meath - September 12, 1861

Delahoyde Surname Ireland: 1600s to 1900s

- George Delahoyde & Eleanor Delahoyde, bur. 10 Oct 1692 (Burial, **St. Michan Parish**)

- James Delahoyde & Sarah Unknown

  o Thomas Delahoyde – bapt. 9 Jan 1754 (Baptism, **St. Werburgh Parish**), bur. 11 Jan 1754

  (Burial, **St. Werburgh Parish**)

Thomas Delahoyde (son):

Age at Death - infant

Cause of Death - small pox

  o Thomas Delahoyde – bapt. May 1758 (Baptism, **St. Werburgh Parish**)

  o Sarah Delahoyde – bapt. 18 Jun 1768 (Baptism, **St. Werburgh Parish**)

James Delahoyde (father):

Residence - Cork Hill - January 9, 1754

May 1758

June 18, 1768

- John Delahoyde & Frances Howard – 27 Sep 1795 (Marriage, **SS. Michael & John Parish** (RC))

- John Delahoyde & Mary Durham – Jul 1764 (Marriage, **St. Michan Parish** (RC))

- John Delahoyde & Unknown

  o Richard Delahoyde & Catherine Monaghan – 29 Feb 1875 (Marriage, **St. James Parish** (RC))

Richard Delahoyde (son):

Residence - 8 Bow Lane - February 29, 1875

Hurst

Catherine Monaghan, daughter of Patrick Monaghan & Unknown (daughter-in-law):

Residence - 8 Bow Lane - February 29, 1875

- Joseph Delahoyde & Margaret Thomson
  - Edward Delahoyde & Anne Fay – 15 Jun 1884 (Marriage, Rathmines Parish (RC))
    - Mary Margaret Delahoyde – b. 22 Apr 1884, bapt. 30 Apr 1884 (Baptism, Rathmines Parish (RC))

Edward Delahoyde (son):

Residence - 3 Clontarf Terrace - June 15, 1884

Harold's Cross - April 30, 1884

Remarks about Marriage - bride entry left blank in church register

- Joseph Delahoyde & Margaret Unknown
  - Joseph Delahoyde & Anne Duffy – 14 May 1874 (Marriage, St. Andrew Parish (RC))
    - Margaret Delahoyde – b. 19 Mar 1878, bapt. 22 Mar 1878 (Baptism, St. Michan Parish (RC))
    - William Delahoyde – b. 30 Jun 1879, bapt. 4 Jul 1879 (Baptism, St. Michan Parish (RC))

Joseph Delahoyde (son):

Residence - Swords - May 14, 1874

13 Anne Street - March 22, 1878

13 North Anne Street - July 4, 1879

Anne Duffy, daughter of James Duffy & Bridget Unknown (daughter-in-law):

Residence - 8 Lower Frederick Street - May 14, 1874

Delahoyde Surname Ireland: 1600s to 1900s

- Michael Delahoyde & Elizabeth Coulter – 20 Oct 1827 (Marriage, **St. Mary Parish**)

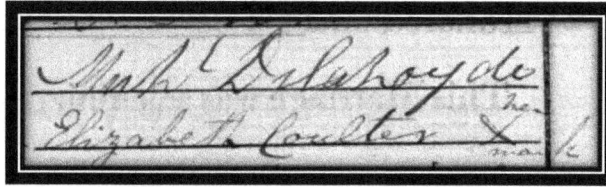

Signatures:

Michael Delahoyde (husband):

Residence - Balraheen Parish, Co. Kildare - October 20, 1827

Elizabeth Coulter (wife):

Residence - St. Mary Parish - October 20, 1827

Wedding Witnesses:

Thomas Mooney & Catherine Lynch

Signatures:

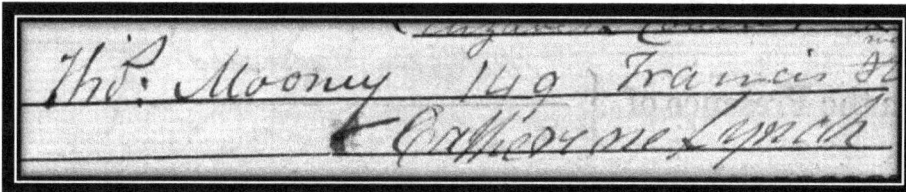

- Patrick Delahoyde & Catherine Wilkinson – 23 Jul 1799 (Marriage, **St. Andrew Parish** (RC))
  - Gulielmo Delahoyde – bapt. 1800 (Baptism, **St. Andrew Parish** (RC))
- Peter Delahoyde & Bridget Morrissey
  - Margaret Mary Delahoyde – b. 27 Jan 1899, bapt. 30 Jan 1899 (Baptism, **St. Mary, Pro Cathedral Parish** (RC))

Hurst

Peter Delahoyde (father):

Residence - 22 Upper Gloucester Street - January 30, 1899

- Pierce Delahoyde & Margaret Boshell

  o Peter Delahoyde – bapt. 12 Jan 1800 (Baptism, **St. Michan Parish (RC)**)

- Richard Delahoyde & Anne Kaine – 10 May 1835 (Marriage, **St. Mary, Pro Cathedral Parish (RC)**)

  o Edward Delahoyde – bapt. 1 Jan 1834 (Baptism, **St. Mary, Pro Cathedral Parish (RC)**)

- Richard Delahoyde & Catherine Kelly – 9 Aug 1787 (Marriage, **St. Catherine Parish (RC)**)

- Richard Delahoyde & Catherine Monahan

  o John Delahoyde – b. 15 Nov 1879, bapt. 21 Nov 1879 (Baptism, **St. Michan Parish (RC)**)

Richard Delahoyde (father):

Residence - 6 Pill Lane - November 21, 1879

- Richard Delahoyde & Sarah Unknown

  o Richard Delahoyde – b. 1746, bapt. 1746 (Baptism, **St. Andrew Parish (RC)**)

  o Michael Delahoyde – bapt. 1753 (Baptism, **St. Andrew Parish (RC)**)

  o James Delahoyde – bapt. 1755 (Baptism, **St. Andrew Parish (RC)**)

  o Edward Delahoyde – bapt. 1759 (Baptism, **St. Andrew Parish (RC)**)

  o Matthew Delahoyde – bapt. 1761 (Baptism, **St. Andrew Parish (RC)**)

- Robert Delahoyde & Margaret Unknown

  o James Delahoyde – bapt. 23 May 1775 (Baptism, **St. James Parish (RC)**)

  o James Delahoyde – bapt. 15 Jun 1775 (Baptism, **St. James Parish (RC)**)

  o Hannah Delahoyde – bapt. 22 Nov 1777 (Baptism, **St. James Parish (RC)**)

Delahoyde Surname Ireland: 1600s to 1900s

- Roger Delahoyde & Mary Unknown

  o Roger Delahoyde – bapt. 28 Feb 1736 (Baptism, **St. Catherine Parish**)

- Timothy Delahoyde & Ellen Kearny (K e a r n y)

  o John Delahoyde – bapt. 26 Jul 1788 (Baptism, **Cork - SS. Peter & Paul Parish (RC)**)

- Thomas Delahoyde & Anne Bolan

  o Edward Delahoyde & Catherine Kilbride – 7 Jan 1859 (Marriage, **St. Catherine Parish (RC)**)

Edward Delahoyde (son):

Residence - 14 Mark's Alley - January 7, 1859

Catherine Kilbride, daughter of Lawrence Kilbride & Anne Graham (daughter-in-law):

Residence - 51 Marrow Bone Lane - January 7, 1859

- Thomas Delahoyde & Judith Unknown

  o Charles Delahoyde – bapt. 26 Mar 1837 (Baptism, **St. Mary, Pro Cathedral Parish (RC)**)

  o Thomas Henry Delahoyde – bapt. 12 Aug 1838 (Baptism, **St. Mary, Pro Cathedral Parish (RC)**)

  o William Patrick Delahoyde – bapt. 28 Mar 1841 (Baptism, **St. Mary, Pro Cathedral Parish (RC)**)

  o Helen Judith Delahoyde – bapt. 20 Aug 1843 (Baptism, **St. Mary, Pro Cathedral Parish (RC)**)

- Thomas Delahoyde & Margaret Field – 4 Nov 1789 (Marriage, **St. Michan Parish (RC)**)

- Thomas Delahoyde & Margaret Unknown

  o Thomas Augustine Delahoyde – bapt. 3 Nov 1805 (Baptism, **St. Mary, Pro Cathedral Parish (RC)**)

Hurst

- Thomas Delahoyde & Martha Unknown

  o Jacques Delahoyde – bapt. 29 Jan 1801 (Baptism, **St. Mary, Pro Cathedral Parish** (RC))

- William Delahoyde & Ursula Unknown

  o Catherine Delahoyde – bapt. 23 May 1726 (Baptism, **St. Michan Parish** (RC))

William Delahoyde (father):

Residence - Ball Lane - May 23, 1726

Individual Baptisms/Births

None Were Listed

Individual Burials

- Eleanor Delahoyde – bur. 30 Jul 1806 (Burial, **St. James Parish**)

Eleanor Delahoyde (deceased):

Residence - Baggot Street - before July 30, 1806

- Elizabeth Delahoyde – b. 1772, bur. 16 Dec 1856 (Burial, **Glasnevin Parish**)

Elizabeth Delahoyde (deceased):

Residence - Power's Court, Lower Deuzille Street, Dublin -

before December 16, 1856

Age at Death - 84 years

- Honor Delahoyde – bur. 21 Jan 1777 (Burial, **St. Luke Parish**)

Honor Delahoyde (deceased):

Residence - Ffordam's Alley - before January 21, 1777

- James Delahoyde – bur. 16 Aug 1785 (Burial, **Paul Parish**)
- John Delahoyde – bur. 4 Jan 1827 (Burial, **St. Nicholas Without Parish**)

John Delahoyde (deceased):

Residence - 60 Kevin's Street - before January 4, 1827

Delahoyde Surname Ireland: 1600s to 1900s

- Margaret Delahoyde – bur. 26 Aug 1816 (Burial, **St. James Parish**)

Margaret Delahoyde (deceased):

    Residence - Balybocle - before August 26, 1816

- Thomas Delahoyde – bur. 3 Jul 1822 (Burial, **St. James Parish**)

Thomas Delahoyde (deceased):

    Residence - Church Street - July 3, 1822

- Unknown Delahoyde – bur. 29 Jun 1807 (Burial, **St. Nicholas Without Parish**)
- Unknown Delahoyde (Miss) – bur. 20 Jul 1807 (Burial, **St. James Parish**)

Unknown Delahoyde (Miss) (deceased):

    Residence - Bridge Street - before July 20, 1807

- Unknown Delahoyde (Mrs.) – b. 1756, bur. 23 Jan 1836 (Burial, **St. Nicholas Parish (RC)**)

Unknown Delahoyde (Mrs.) (deceased):

    Residence - Rathmines - before January 23, 1836

    Age at Death - 80 years

- William Delahoyde – bur. 21 Jul 1816 (Burial, **St. James Parish**)

William Delahoyde (deceased):

    Residence - Beahan's Town - before July 21, 1816

Individual Marriages

- Anne Delahoyde & Cornelius (C o r n e l i u s) O'Leary

  o Mary O'Leary – bapt. 26 Jun 1794 (Baptism, **St. Michan Parish** (RC))

- Anne Delahoyde & Patrick Flannagan

  o Thomas Flannagan – bapt. 15 Dec 1807 (Baptism, **St. Catherine Parish** (RC))

  o Elizabeth Flannagn – bapt. 22 Apr 1810 (Baptism, **St. Catherine Parish** (RC))

  o Anne Flannagan – bapt. 27 Jul 1817 (Baptism, **St. Catherine Parish** (RC))

- Bridget Delahoyde & James Leonard – 9 Sep 1790 (Baptism, **St. Andrew Parish** (RC))

- Catherine Delahoyde & George Beahan

  o Elizabeth Beahan & Gulielmo Lawlor – 11 Jan 1881 (Marriage, **St. Mary, Haddington Road Parish** (RC))

Elizabeth Beahan (daughter):

Residence - 36 Pembroke Road - January 11, 1881

Gulielmo Lawlor, son of Gulielmo Lawlor & Anne Unknown (son-in-law):

Residence - Larkvale - January 11, 1881

- Catherine Delahoyde & Nicholas Sinnot – 4 Dec 1632 (Marriage, **St. John Parish**)

- Elizabeth Delahoyde & Joseph O'Brien

  o John O'Brien & Mary Dalton – 25 Sep 1898 (Marriage, **Harrington Street Parish** (RC))

Delahoyde Surname Ireland: 1600s to 1900s

John O'Brien (son):

> Residence - Skerries, Co. Dublin - September 25, 1898

Mary Dalton, daughter of Dennis Dalton & Jane Murphy (daughter-in-law):

> Residence - 7 Lower Clanbrassil - September 25, 1898

- Ellen Delahoyde & John Love
  - Henry Love – bapt. 19 Jul 1795 (Baptism, **Cork - SS. Peter & Paul Parish (RC)**)

John Love (father):

> Residence - Coal Quay - July 19, 1795

- Emily Delahoyde & Patrick Box
  - Mary Frances Box – b. 19 Oct 1877, bapt. 22 Oct 1877 (Baptism, **St. Lawrence Parish (RC)**)
  - Josephine Mary Box – b. 29 Nov 1879, bapt. 1 Dec 1879 (Baptism, **St. Lawrence Parish (RC)**)
  - Francis Thomas Box – b. 21 Aug 1883, bapt. 24 Aug 1883 (Baptism, **St. Agatha Parish (RC)**)

Patrick Box (father):

> Residence - 7 Hawthorn Terrace, Church Road - October 22, 1877

> 15 Erne Terrace - December 1, 1879

> 29 Russell Avenue - August 24, 1883

- Mary Delahoyde & Francis Marmion (M a r m i o n)
  - Anthony Marmion (M a r m i o n) – bapt. 3 Jul 1800 (Baptism, **St. Michan Parish (RC)**)
  - Mary Marmion (M a r m i o n) – bapt. 3 Jun 1802 (Baptism, **St. Michan Parish (RC)**)

Hurst

- Mary Delahoyde & Matthew Kelch

  o Catherine Kelch & John Croar – 18 May 1862 (Marriage, **St. Catherine Parish** (RC))

Catherine Kelch (daughter):

    Residence - 6 Ormond Street - May 18, 1862

John Croar, son of John Croar & Margaret Connor (son-in-law):

    Residence - 11 Marrow Bone Lane - May 18, 1862

- Mary Delahoyde & Matthew Francis Tighe

  o Peter Joseph Tighe – b. 1859, bapt. 1859 (Baptism, **Clondalkin Parish** (RC))

  o Francis Thomas Tighe – b. 1860, bapt. 1860 (Baptism, **Clondalkin Parish** (RC))

  o Matthew Tighe – b. 1863, bapt. 1863 (Baptism, **Clondalkin Parish** (RC))

  o Mary Josephine Tighe, b. 1865, bapt. 1865 (Baptism, **Clondalkin Parish** (RC)) & Simon Woods

     – 24 Apr 1884 (Marriage, **Clondalkin Parish** (RC))

Mary Tighe (daughter):

    Residence - Clondalkin - April 24, 1884

Simon Woods, son of Andrew Woods & Anne Woods (son-in-law):

    Residence - Lower Clonborris - April 24, 1884

  o David Robert Tighe – b. 1867, bapt. 1867 (Baptism, **Clondalkin Parish** (RC))

  o William Joseph Tighe – b. 1869, bapt. 1869 (Baptism, **Clondalkin Parish** (RC))

  o Emily Margaret Tighe – b. 1871, bapt. 1871 (Baptism, **Clondalkin Parish** (RC))

  o Josephine Mary Tighe – b. 1873, bapt. 1873 (Baptism, **Clondalkin Parish** (RC))

  o Teresa Mary Tighe – b. 1875, bapt. 1875 (Baptism, **Clondalkin Parish** (RC))

Delahoyde Surname Ireland: 1600s to 1900s

Matthew Francis Tighe (father):

Residence - 9th Lock, Clondalkin - 1859

1860

1873

1875

Neilstown - 1863

1865

1867

1869

1871

- Mary Delahoyde & Nicholas Stokes

  o Sophie Stokes – bapt. 1783 (Baptism, **SS. Michael & John Parish (RC)**)

  o Mary Stokes – bapt. 1784 (Baptism, **St. Andrew Parish (RC)**)

- Mary Anne Delahoyde & Patrick Doyle

  o John Doyle – b. 19 Feb 1873, bapt. 24 Feb 1873 (Baptism, **St. Mary, Pro Cathedral Parish (RC)**)

  o Catherine Mary Doyle – b. 19 Feb 1875, bapt. 22 Feb 1875 (Baptism, **St. Mary, Pro Cathedral Parish (RC)**)

Patrick Doyle (father):

Residence - 19 Lower Mecklenburgh Street - February 24, 1873

93 Lower Mecklenburgh Street - February 22, 1875

Hurst

- Mary Anne Delahoyde & Richard Cartan

  o Richard Paul Cartan – bapt. 3 Jul 1836 (Baptism, **Rathmines Parish (RC)**)

Delahoyde Surname Ireland: 1600s to 1900s

Name Variations

Includes Latin and Abbreviated forms of names found in the original documents.

Abigail = Abigale, Abigall

Anne = Ann, Anna, Annae

Bartholomew = Barth, Bartholmeus, Bartholomeo

Bridget = Birgis, Brigid, Brigida, Bridgit

Catherine = Catharine, Catharina, Catharinae, Catherina, Cath, Catha, Cathae, Cathe, Cathn, Kate

Charles = Carolus, Charls, Chas

Christopher = Christoph

Daniel = Danielem, Danielis

Edmund = Edmond

Edward = Ed, Edwd

Eleanor = Eleo, Eleonora, Elinor, Ellenor

Elizabeth = Betty, Elisa, Elisabeth, Eliz, Eliza, Elizab, Elizh, Elizth

Ellen = Elena, Ellena

Emily = Emilia

Esther = Essie, Ester

Francis = Fransicum

George = Geo, Georg, Georgius

Grace = Gratiae

Gulielmo = Guil, Guillelmi, Gulielmum, Guillelmus, Gulmi

Delahoyde Surname Ireland: 1600s to 1900s

Helen = Helena

Honor = Hanora, Honora

James = Jacobi, Jacobus, Jas

Jane = Joanna

Jeanne = Jeannae, Joannae

Joan = Johanna, Joney

John = Jno, Joannem, Joannes, Johannis

Joseph = Jos

Juliana = Julian

Leticia = Letitia, Lettice, Letticia

Lewis = Louis

Luke = Lucas

Margaret = Margarita, Margaritae, Margeret, Marget, Margt

Martha = Marthae

Mary = Maria, My

Mary Anne = Marianna, Marianne, Maryanne

Michael = Michaelis, Michl

Patrick = Pat, Patt, Patk, Patricii, Patricius

Peter = Petri

Richard = Ricardi, Ricardus, Rich, Richd

Robert = Roberti

Rose = Rosa, Rosae

Thomas = Thom, Thomae, Thoms, Thos, Ths

Timothy = Timotheus, Timy

William = Wil, Will, Willm, Wm

Notes

Notes

Notes

Notes

Notes

Notes

Index

B

C

Delahoyde Surname Ireland: 1600s to 1900s

D

Delahoyde Surname Ireland: 1600s to 1900s

About The Author

Donovan Hurst graduated from San Diego State University with a Bachelor of Arts in the major field of studies of History and a minor in the field of studies of Anthropology. He is a current member of The General Society of Mayflower Descendants and has been conducting genealogical research for over 10 years tracing back his ancestors to their ancestral homelands in Denmark, England, France, Germany, Ireland, Norway, and Scotland.